DIGITAL PHOTO
MADNESS!

DIGITAL PHOTO
MADNESS!

50 Weird & Wacky Things to Do
with your Digital Camera

THOM GAINES

LARK BOOKS

A Division of Sterling Publishing Co., Inc.
New York

Library of Congress Cataloging-in-Publication Data

Gaines, Thom, 1973-
  Digital photo madness : 50 weird & wacky things to do with your digital
camera / by Thom Gaines.
       p. cm.
  Includes index.
  ISBN 1-57990-624-9 (pbk.)
  1. Photography—Digital techniques. 2. Digital cameras. I. Title.
TR267.G35 2006
775—dc22

                                              2005034365

10 9 8 7 6 5 4 3 2

Published by Lark Books, A Division of
Sterling Publishing Co., Inc.
387 Park Avenue South, New York, N.Y. 10016

© 2006, Thom Gaines

Distributed in Canada by Sterling Publishing,
c/o Canadian Manda Group, 165 Dufferin Street
Toronto, Ontario, Canada M6K 3H6

Distributed in the United Kingdom by GMC Distribution Services,
Castle Place, 166 High Street, Lewes, East Sussex, England BN7 1XU

Distributed in Australia by Capricorn Link (Australia) Pty Ltd.,
P.O. Box 704, Windsor, NSW 2756 Australia

If you have questions or comments about this book, please contact:
Lark Books
67 Broadway
Asheville, NC 28801
(828) 253-0467

Manufactured in China

ISBN 13: 978-1-57990-624-5
ISBN 10: 1-57990-624-9

Editor: Rain Newcomb
Art Director and Cover Designer: Thom Gaines
Creative Director: Celia Naranjo
Editorial Assistance: Delores Gosnell

For information about custom editions, special
sales, premium and corporate purchases, please
contact Sterling Special Sales Department at
800-805-5489 or specialsales@sterlingpub.com.

CONTENTS

INTRODUCTION

If you're like me, you already know digital photography is the best invention ever. Two words: instant gratification! You can see what you've shot

immediately and delete any bad pictures you've taken before anyone sees them. You can print only your best photos, email them, or post them on a website. And the very best part is the crazy stuff you can do with your digital pictures on your computer.

Learn how to take awesome action shots (Ch. 2), and then learn how to combine your photos (Ch. 8).

How to Use This Book

Whether you've just taken your first digital camera out of the box or you've been shooting for years, you'll find information, tips, and tricks in this book that will take your digital photography to a whole new level.

You can begin now—anywhere you like. Flip through the chapters, find a subject that intrigues you, and give it a whirl. If you need to know something that I've already explained, the page references will tell you where to find the information. If you see a word in blue, you can look it up in the glossary at the back of the book.

Most of the hands-on information can be found in two types of boxes:

IN THE FIELD

The gray boxes give you instructions and tips for taking awesome shots.

IN THE LAB

The blue boxes help you use software to make your photo even better.

This footbridge is a superb subject (Ch. 6).
It also has great color and lighting (Ch. 3).

This macro shot (Ch. 5) has interesting
lines and composition (Ch. 4).

I'm still laughing at the crazy shots I
took this summer in mirrors (Ch. 7).

Use this book for inspiration and
guidance, and then go out and have
fun. (Experimentation will teach you
more than any book—except maybe
this one.) So charge your batteries,
leave plenty of room on your memory
card, and keep your eyes open for the
next great shot.

Chapter 1 **Digital Basics** explains what
a digital photo is, what the buttons on your
camera do, how the digital process works, and
how to use photo software.

Chapter 2 **Camera Tricks** will help you learn
how and when to use all those fancy buttons, dials,
bells, and whistles on your camera.

Chapter 3 **Color & Light** shows you how to
use—you guessed it—color and light to make
your photos pop.

Chapter 4 **Composition** will show you how to
set-up shots and develop other skills that will make
you a fantastic photographer.

Chapter 5 **Macrotopia** brings you to a whole
new world—the world of close-up photography.
You'll find some ideas for taking really whacky shots
of insects, flowers, people, and more.

Chapter 6 **Superb Subjects** gives you tips
and inspiration for shooting your favorite subjects.
From yourself to your pet, from the museum to the
aquarium, you'll find some great things to shoot..

Chapter 7 **Phunky Fotos** gets crazy with
some wild shots. Use mirrors, buildings, water,
and more to create crazy photos.

Chapter 8 **Altered Reality** is where the
madness really takes over. Edit, combine, and
alter your digital photos to make awesome
pictures that'll impress your friends and make
you laugh out loud.

digital basics

...because you can never know too much about using your camera and software.

THE DIGITAL PROCESS

The digital process is very flexible. You can have your images professionally printed at a store kiosk (path A) or transfer them to your computer (path B) where you can *be* the photo lab. The creative possibilities are endless!

Load a memory card into the camera

Most cameras store their files on memory cards that can be removed. The more memory you have, the more photos you can take. Memory cards come in different sizes and shapes. Use the one that's right for your camera.

Take cool photos

This book gives you lots of great ideas. Then choose a path for your next step.

path **A**

path **B**

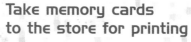

Take memory cards to the store for printing

Using an onscreen menu, you can choose which photos to print and how big they'll be. To see how large you can print your digital photo, see the chart on page 124. Burn your images to a CD for backup.

Make cool stuff

Use your software to create calendars, slideshows, webpages, and much more. Go crazy altering and combining your images. Some great ideas are in this book.

Print at home

A variety of home printers can print your images on photographic paper, business cards, magnets, puzzles, and more.

Transfer images to your computer

Hook a USB cable from your camera to your computer to access your photos. Then use photo software to transfer, edit, and organize your collection of photos (pg. 18).

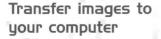

Transfer images directly from your memory card to the computer using a card reader. Your memory card will work like a disk.

EXPLORE YOUR CAMERA

Every camera is capable of taking great photos. To get the best pictures possible from your digital camera, you need to know what it can do. That means learning *how* and *when* to use all the features.

Take a look at some common features and functions explained here, and then revisit your own camera to see what it has to offer. You might even want to read the manual.

The Camera Body

Don't be afraid...push every button and see what happens. Experimentation is a great way to learn.

Ready Lights
Give you the green light when your flash is ready.

Optical Viewfinder
Use this instead of the LCD screen to conserve battery life.

Zoom Controls
Zoom out to wide angle or zoom in to telephoto.

LCD Screen
Use as a viewfinder to frame shots or as a viewscreen to preview photos. Using the screen drains battery life.

Wrist Strap
Always make your friends wear this when they're using your camera.

Special buttons
Change between Flash and Macro modes. Set the timer delay.

Menu Controls
Access the programmable features of your camera. Review and delete photos in Preview mode.

Camera Mode Selection Wheel
Select Automatic, Program, or Scene modes (pg. 13). Switch to Preview or Movie mode.

Memory Card
More memory allows more pictures.

Card Slot Door
Access your memory card or plug in special cords.

Camera Modes

Programming your camera doesn't have to be difficult. You can have more fun with your camera and take better pictures by using some simple features. See what your camera can do, then get out there and start taking photos.

Manual Mode
You have full control, including exposure. Now you're the expert!*

Scene Modes
Use these settings to shoot specific types of shots. (See Chapter 2 for examples.) Types may include:
- Action shots
- Landscapes
- Portraits
- Night shots and candlelight
- Snow scenes

Program Mode
You can make some adjustments (see box below), but the camera will handle the exposure.

Fully Automatic Mode
Just point and shoot. If your photo doesn't come out the way you want, try switching to program mode and start experimenting.

Preview Mode
Use the viewscreen to check out your photos.

Movie Mode
Make small digital movies. It uses a lot of memory and battery power.

* Using full manual modes (M), including (A) Aperture and (S) Shutter priority, is beyond the scope of this book. Please consult your manual to learn more about these modes.

COMMON PROGRAMMING FEATURES

Focus mode (A) can change between Auto Focus and Manual Distance focusing modes (pg. 68).

Flash strength (A) can increase or decrease the power of the flash. Lower the power for close shots, increase the power for distance (pgs. 48 through 51).

ISO settings give you a choice of film-speed equivalents (100, 200, 400, or 800 speed). 100–200 speed is better for daylight shooting and for use with the flash. 400–800 speed is better for action shots and for photos in low light situations when you don't want to use the flash.

White balance (B) adjusts the camera to different lighting conditions that may discolor your images (pgs. 29 and 30).

Exposure compensation (C) adjusts the amount of light in a photo. For over-exposed images that look too light and cloudy, lower the exposure. For under-exposed images that look too dark, raise the exposure.

ACCESSORIES FOR THE FIELD

There's nothing worse than having the perfect photographic moment and being unable to take the shot. Having a couple of items in your possession can ensure that you're always prepared.

Camera Bag

Don't let your stuff get beat up or rained on out in the field. Get a good camera bag that's small enough to carry anywhere but big enough to store and protect your supplies. With the bag shown on the left, you could put your mini-tripod in the front pocket and your spare batteries and memory cards in the side pockets.

Extra Batteries & a Charger

You'll find that most digital cameras eat batteries like you eat candy. Fast and furious. Always have more batteries around other than the ones in your camera. Rechargeable batteries can save you lots of money, and there are pocket-sized rechargers for them that will fit in your camera bag. If you know you've only got one set left, practice the battery-saving techniques below.

Go with name-brand batteries you can trust. You might think you're getting a good deal on those no-name batteries, but think again. They've been sitting in a warehouse for five years!

IN THE FIELD

Conserve Battery Life

■ Turn off the viewscreen and take your photos with the viewfinder.

■ Don't use the flash unless it's absolutely necessary.

■ No previewing. Tell your friends that they can see their goofy picture later!

■ Save the moviemaking or voice recording for later. They use more battery life than pictures.

Tripods come in many sizes and shapes. Get one that's portable, but make sure it can support your camera.

Tripods

For most daylight and flash situations, hand-holding your camera will produce good shots. However, there are some times when a good tripod will come in handy.

You'll need to stabilize your camera whenever you take a long exposure, such as with night photography (pg. 28) or Soft Flash mode (pg. 51). If you move the camera during a long exposure, your picture will be blurry. This is known as camera shake. Most cameras will warn you of possible camera shake before you take the photo. (Watch out for a flashing icon ((🖐)) on the viewscreen.) Follow the steps below to avoid blurry pictures.

IN THE FIELD

Preventing Camera Shake ((🖐))

Learning to be a human tripod takes practice, but the results are worth it.

▣ Use a tripod and the Timer Delay ⟳. (Even on a tripod, pushing the shutter button can shake the camera.)

▣ If you don't have a tripod, rest your camera on a flat surface. Turn on the Timer Delay ⟳ and use the viewscreen to focus and frame the shot. Push the shutter button and step away from the camera.

▣ If you have to hold the camera to take the photo, put your elbows at your sides and hold the camera close to your body (see photo). Focus on the subject, but wait until you breathe out to take the shot. Practice this technique—you'll need it at the museum (pg. 86).

THE RESOLUTION SOLUTION

Nothing is more mind-boggling than understanding image resolution. Have you ever tried to load a webpage that took forever to display? Or have you ever printed a huge family photo only to find that mom's head is made of 15 blurry squares? These are both problems of resolution. Unfortunately, there's only one solution—read and learn.

Pixels
The building blocks digital images.

Pixels

The word pixel stands for Picture Element and refers to the smallest building block of digital images. Digital cameras *capture* images as pixels and computer monitors *display* pixels. Pixels are actually tiny dots of light, arranged in a grid of vertical and horizontal rows. Color is a property of light, so each pixel can be any color of the rainbow. When seen together, pixels combine to form images, text, icons, and even movies on your computer screen.

4.1 MEGAPIXELS
MPEGMOVIE VX

MEGAPIXELS

It takes thousands, even *millions* of pixels, to print a good-sized photograph. That's why today's cameras are measured in megapixels, or millions of pixels. Select a high megapixel setting if you want to make large prints and get the most detail possible. Select a lower megapixel setting to save on memory and take more photos. See the chart on page 124 to find out exactly how many mega-pixels your camera records and how big a picture you can print.

16 pixels
1 inch

|◄——— 16 dpi ———►|

Resolution

In order for our eyes to see images instead of dots, pixels on a monitor have to be very small. Most monitors display 72 dots of light per horizontal or vertical inch. This measurement describes the monitor's resolution, and is measured in dpi or *dots per inch*.

Intended use	Resolution
Computer screen	72dpi
Adequate Print Quality	150 dpi
Good Quality Print	200 dpi
Excellent Quality Print	250+ dpi

72 dpi is a good resolution to display dots of light on a computer screen, but it's not high enough to print dots of ink on paper to make a good quality photograph. To see what your resolution should be for printed photographs, see the chart above.

|◄——— 6 inches @ 341 dpi ———►|

|◄——————— 10 inches @ 205 dpi ———————►|

Scaling Digital Images

Scaling, or changing the physical size of a digital image, also changes the resolution. Size and resolution have what is called an inverse relationship—when size goes up, resolution goes down and vice versa.

For instance, let's say you place an image with a 2048 x 1365 pixel size into a page layout program and it appears at 6 x 4 inches. It would have a resolution of 341 pixels/inch because 2048 pixels/6 inches = 341 pixels/inch. If you were to scale the image larger to 10 inches wide the resolution would decrease to 2048 pixels/10 inches, or 205 pixels per inch. The resolution decreases because you are stretching the same amount of pixels over a greater area.

DIGITAL PHOTO SOFTWARE

There's a new breed of photo software specifically designed to use with digital cameras. It helps you organize your photo albums, view and edit images, and even make cool stuff like calendars and picture books. Chances are, your camera probably came with one of these software packages. You can use it for many of the **IN THE LAB** sections of this book.

Import Photos
Add photos to your library from your camera and from folders on your computer.

Create
Create books, movies, and webpages from your photo albums.

Share
Prepare an image for emailing or IM-ing.

Quick Fix
This button adjusts your image for optimum color and contrast.

Print
Print photos and contact sheets.

Timeline
Quickly navigate through your photo collection.

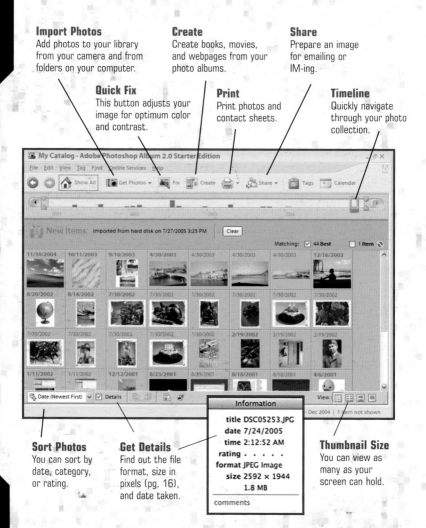

Sort Photos
You can sort by date, category, or rating.

Get Details
Find out the file format, size in pixels (pg. 16), and date taken.

Information

title DSC05253.JPG
date 7/24/2005
time 2:12:52 AM
rating . . . . .
format JPEG Image
size 2592 × 1944
1.8 MB

comments

Thumbnail Size
You can view as many as your screen can hold.

Basic Photo Tools

Double-click on a photo to open it for editing, then use your mouse to accomplish a variety of tasks. Heck, this is so easy even your parents can do it.

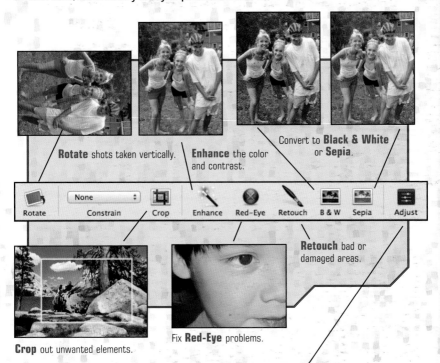

Rotate shots taken vertically.

Enhance the color and contrast.

Convert to **Black & White** or **Sepia**.

Rotate	Constrain	None	Crop	Enhance	Red-Eye	Retouch	B & W	Sepia	Adjust

Retouch bad or damaged areas.

Crop out unwanted elements.

Fix **Red-Eye** problems.

Manual Controls

A good photo software package will give you a variety of ways to change your picture. This window, from Apple's iPhoto software, allows you to fine-tune your photograph. You'll be using similar controls for some of the projects in this book.

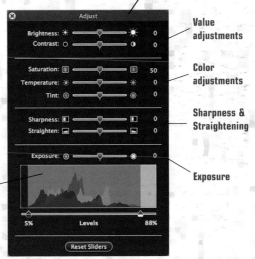

Value adjustments

Color adjustments

Sharpness & Straightening

Exposure

Adjust		
Brightness:		0
Contrast:		0
Saturation:		50
Temperature:		0
Tint:		0
Sharpness:		0
Straighten:		0
Exposure:		0

5%   Levels   88%

(Reset Sliders)

Levels

A window for adjusting the color levels in your photograph is an excellent feature.

ADVANCED PHOTO SOFTWARE

Step up to what the professionals use and unleash your creative potential. This software is relatively inexpensive considering how much you can do with it back in the lab. We'll do some killer stuff with it in Chapter 8. You'll be able to use the software that came with your camera for most of the book.

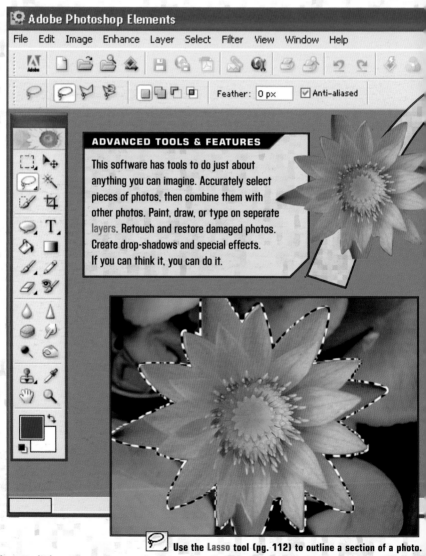

Adobe Photoshop Elements

File   Edit   Image   Enhance   Layer   Select   Filter   View   Window   Help

Feather: 0 px   ☑ Anti-aliased

ADVANCED TOOLS & FEATURES

This software has tools to do just about anything you can imagine. Accurately select pieces of photos, then combine them with other photos. Paint, draw, or type on seperate layers. Retouch and restore damaged photos. Create drop-shadows and special effects. If you can think it, you can do it.

Use the Lasso tool (pg. 112) to outline a section of a photo.

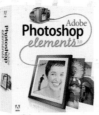

Three very capable advanced software packages are:

Corel **Paint Shop Pro**
Ulead **PhotoImpact**
Adobe **Photoshop Elements***

*I used Adobe software for the advanced projects in the book.

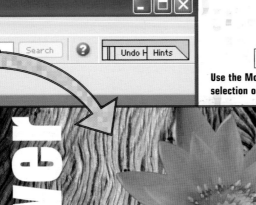

Use the Move tool to drag the selection on top of another image.

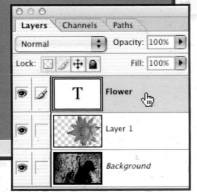

Layers

Images and text can be kept on seperate layers, allowing you to move, scale, and rotate them independently. Create as many layers as you want, and blend them together with special effects.

camera tricks

...where you'll use
your camera's features
to take awesome
photographs.

oto ▷

madness

PORTRAITS & PEOPLE

Taking a good portrait requires patience and an element of surprise. A natural, unplanned facial expression is what you're looking for, and most people won't give you that if they know there's a camera pointing at them. Be patient. Just keep them in focus until that magic moment when they crack open and reveal their true selves.

Kids are great for portraits because they're always smiling.

Portrait Mode

Switch to Portrait mode 🔲 for all your daytime head shots. This ensures that the background will be out of focus and less of a competing factor with the real subject—the face.

For taking portraits indoors or at night, use the Night Portrait mode 🔲. This will most likely use a soft flash setting (pg. 51).

A standard portrait is of the head and shoulders, but you can vary it as you like. For tips on composing photos, see Chapter 4.

The eyes are the most expressive part of the face. Sometimes they may be hard to read, but they are definitely saying something.

IN THE FIELD

Expressive Portraits

Your portraits don't have to be of smiling faces. Sometimes portraits can express other emotions, like loneliness, frustration, or desire. Changes in facial expression are so subtle and so quick, you'll find there's a real art to catching these hidden emotions. (For help with shooting in Black & White or Sepia, see pages 40 through 43.)

When taking photos of more than one person, be creative and direct your subjects into non-standard poses. You'll find that it takes a bit of assertiveness, but the results will be worth it.

PERFECT LANDSCAPES

Perhaps the hardest part of taking an awesome landscape photo is finding the perfect location. You have to get out of the house and explore the world. Walk the streets. Hike that trail. Sooner or later, you'll be in the presence of something special. Once you're there, the rest is a snap.

A great time to shoot landscapes is in the late afternoon, when the sun casts interesting shadows (pg. 46).

IN THE FIELD

1 Set your camera to Landscape mode ▲. This ensures a long depth of field (see the next page).

2 Focus on the closest area of interest. However, if you want your background to be in focus, don't focus on anything within an arms length of the camera. In the shot above it would be good to focus on the orange building in the foreground.

3 Stabilize your camera (pg. 15) before taking the shot.

IN THE FIELD

Depth of Field

With most landscape shots, you'll want everything in the frame to be in focus, whether it's in the foreground or miles away. This is what photographers call a *long* depth of field. To achieve a long depth of field, the opening in the lens, or aperture, must be very small.

It takes your camera more time to record an image using a small aperture—and this could mean camera shake. That's why most landscape photographers use a tripod (pg. 15).

If you're in a situation like this, switch to Landscape mode [▲▲] and focus halfway up the tree.

Some cameras come with a Beach Landscape mode [☀] that captures the the rich blue and green colors at the beach.

NIGHT LIFE

No photographer's portfolio is complete without a great night shot. Technically, it's not that difficult once you've got an awesome location and subject—the most important factor is keeping the camera still while you're taking the photo. With a little preparation, you'll be out on the town and able to bring home the night.

IN THE FIELD

1 Find an awesome location to record a night scene.

2 Set your camera to Night mode 🌙 and turn off the flash ⚡.

3 Stabilize your camera. Use a tripod or rest the camera on a flat surface (pg. 15).

4 Set the Timer Delay ⏱. Focus on your subject and frame the picture.

5 Fully press the shutter button, then remove your hand from the camera. Wait for the timer to count down and take the picture.

6 Preview ▶ the shot and zoom in 🔍 to check the focus.

If your camera doesn't have Night mode, take the photo in Landscape mode ⛰. Use the exposure compensation and white balance settings to make adjustments.

For tips on holding
the camera steady
without a tripod,
see page 15.

IN THE FIELD

White Balance

In the photo above, the brightest highlights have a yellow
tint from the incandescent/tungsten light source. The photo
to the right has a blue tint from the flourescent light source.
If your camera has it, you can use the white balance settings to correct the color by specifying the light source.
If you like the moody effect, don't mess with it.

Teletubbies are only spooky
in low-light situations.

The State Fair is a great place to capture a night scene.

SNOW WHITE, NOT GRAY

In order to record good highlights and shadows in the same shot, your camera must choose an exposure between the two. This mid gray level works for most photos, but what happens if most of your subject matter is bright white, like in snow scenes? You might have guessed it from the title—gray snow. Hey, at least it's not yellow. Here's how to keep your whites bright.

These tips work well for other all-white subjects, such as this rose.

IN THE FIELD

Snow How

Some newer cameras come with an automatic Snow mode 🔲 that corrects the exposure and color saturation before you shoot, but you can also make the adjustments manually on your camera (see below) or on your computer in the lab (see the next page).

1 Use the viewscreen on your camera to frame your shot and access the program settings.

2 Find the exposure compensation setting ⊡ and adjust it in the positive direction to brighten your image.

3 When the snow turns white without losing much saturation in the other color areas, take the shot.

These hard-core snow trekkers encountered more than bright white conditions. They also had to cross the mysterious blue ice.

Snow Cleaning

This is one case I found where the automatic color enhancement does a really good job. I tried to achieve the same results on my own, but I wasn't as successful as the computer. If this thing gets any smarter, I'll have to pull the plug!

Enhance

1 Find the auto-enhance feature of your software and give it a try.

2 If you're not pleased with the results, **Edit / Undo** and move to the manual controls (and don't be surprised if you can't do any better).

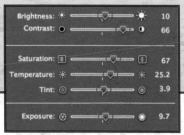

Brightness:	10
Contrast:	66
Saturation:	67
Temperature:	25.2
Tint:	3.9
Exposure:	9.7

Sometimes, you just have to let the computer win.

ACTION REACTION!

Taking action shots is challenging, but super fun. You'll need lots of memory space on your card and a spoonful of patience—getting the perfect action shot takes practice.

IN THE FIELD

3... 2... 1... Jump!

1 Switch your camera to Action mode and get a person or group of people to stand in the sunlight. For more impact, choose an angle where the background will be in shade.

2 Come up with a countdown sequence so that everyone goes airborne at the same time.

3 Pre-focus on your subjects by pressing the shutter button half-way down. Start the countdown and take the photo when your subjects are flying high.

> If your action photo is a little blurry, try re-shooting with the flash on.

Faceplant! Do you have a friend who does a perfect bellyflop? Just make sure you don't get water on your camera.

Speedy Gonzales

1 Find a location where you know something will come speeding by, such as a bicycle race.

2 Set your camera to Landscape mode 🏔 and focus on a midway point between you and the background.

3 When the action comes speeding by, hold very still and fully press the shutter button. Whoosh—it was all a blur.

And the winner is? Whoops, I can't tell, but it sure is a fantastic photo.

MULTIPLE FRAMES

Some cameras can capture the action of fast moving subjects in multiple frame bursts. Record the final seconds of a race or a gymnast flying through the air. Print your shots as a sequence or use advanced photo software to combine them into one killer image.

IN THE FIELD

Action Burst

1 Switch to Program mode and change from Single Frame ☐ to Burst mode ⌧.

2 Stabilize your camera on a flat surface or a tripod (pg. 15).

3 Pre-focus on the area where the action will take place (pg. 33).

4 Fully press the shutter button when the action comes your way. The camera should take a series of photos.

Read the section of your camera manual on Burst mode. You may have other programmable options, like changing how many shots it will take in a row.

For this series of photos at the skating rink, I combined Burst mode ⌧ with Night mode ☽ (pg. 28).

IN THE LAB

All Together Now

If you have advanced photo software (pg. 20), you can kick the coolness factor up a notch by combining the three photos into one. Here's how.

1 Open all three photos and arrange them in order on your screen. We'll refer to them as photos **A**, **B**, and **C**.

2 Click on photo B. Choose **Select / All** from the top menu. Then choose **Edit / Copy** (see below).

3 Click on photo **A** and choose **Edit / Paste**. This puts photo **B** on a layer over photo **A** (see the Layers window above).

4 Repeat steps 2 and 3 for photo **C**. It should become Layer 2.

5 The last step is to change the Layer Blending mode of both layers to Screen. This allows all the layers to blend together. Awesome!

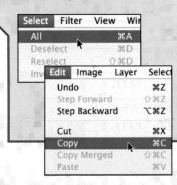

color & light

...in which you'll play with the two essential elements of photography.

oto

madness

COLOR COMBOS

Colors often look best when they're next to other colors. In fact, there's a whole science behind how to combine colors to achieve eye-pleasing combinations (ask any interior designer or flower gardener). But as a person who just wants to record a great photo, you just need to tune your senses to the amazing possibilities of color.

The different shades of color produced by the light and shadow falling on these walls makes for a wild abstract photo.

The pastel color of this wall is a perfect complement to Kim's skin tone and clothing.

IN THE FIELD

Looking for Color

1 Find an interesting color grouping and set your camera to the appropriate Scene mode and white balance setting (pg. 13). The photo above was shot in Landscape mode 🔺 with a Full Sun setting. The photo to the left was shot in Portrait mode 👤 with a Shade or Cloudy setting.

2 Compose your photo. For tips on composition, see Chapter 4.

3 Preview ▶ your image. If you need to make changes, adjust your camera settings as necessary.

A Custom Tint

Change the mood of this photo by playing with the color and saturation. The end result looks like a faded photograph from grandpa's shoebox of summer-camp memories.

1 Open your image and click on the manual Adjustment control (pg. 19).

Adjust

2 Adjust the Hue slider to shift all the colors in the spectrum. (Hue is another word for color.) Slide it around until you like the color change.

3 Move the Saturation slider toward the negative end. This removes the color information and softens the impact of the photo.

Hue:	−168
Saturation:	0
Lightness:	0

Hue:	−168
Saturation:	−62
Lightness:	0

A change in hue and saturation can drastically alter the perception of an image.

BLACK & WHITE

Old cars with chrome bumpers make great subjects for Black & White photos.

In the old days, everyone studying art photography shot with Black & White film. It was easier to process than color photography, so students could develop and print their own photos in a darkroom. —Old School! Now you can be *artsy-fartsy* with just a click of a button. Here's how to do it **IN THE FIELD** or **IN THE LAB**.

IN THE FIELD

Art Shot

1 Switch your camera to Black & White mode (pg. 83). If your camera doesn't have this mode, shoot in color and convert the picture in the lab (see next page).

2 Find a good subject or setting with lots of contrast between light and dark areas. If it's cloudy, wait for the sun to cast some nice shadows.

3 Frame the shot and take the picture.

From Color to Black & White

Some software can convert a color image to Black & White with a touch of a button. If you don't see a button, you can also remove the color by lowering the saturation adjustment (pg. 19).

Saturation:	-100

This Chinese statue made an excellent choice for Black & White because of its contrasting light and dark areas.

Before I switched to Black & White photography, I was just a computer geek. Now I'm an *artiste*.

SEPIA

In the early days of photography, a chemical was applied to Black & White photos to keep them from fading. This turned them rust colored, but ensured

their survival for many long years. Now, many cameras can simulate the old look of Sepia tones without the messy chemicals. You can also create the effect in the lab.

In the early days of photography, people had to hold very still in front of the camera. Any movement would result in a blurry mess. That's why everyone looks so serious.

IN THE FIELD

Old-Fashioned Photo Shoot

Gather some ancient fashions from the local thrift store, then set-up your own old-timey photo shoot. Look for these items:

- spectacles
- long white gloves
- shiny black shoes
- bow ties
- stuff with lace
- a fake moustache
- anything that smells like it's been in an attic for decades.

Next you'll need to find a simple and timeless background. Don't forget to take off your iPod.

Coach everyone in the photo to make a relaxed facial expression and not smile—this will make your antique shot even more authentic. If you want to be in the shot, set up a tripod and use the Timer Delay ⏱ (pg. 15).

Convert to Sepia

Some software can convert an image to Sepia with a touch of a button. If you don't see a button, you can also change to Sepia using the following adjustments.

1 If you're using basic software, find the Temperature and Tint sliders. Slide them both toward the warm red colors. Next, move the Saturation slider down and voilà—the rust-colored photo we're aiming for.

2 If you're using an advanced program, you can achieve the same results by adjusting the hue and saturation controls. Check the colorize box or your photo will turn out like the project on page 39.

Taking your picture in Sepia will not get you your driver's license any sooner!

SEE THE LIGHT (OR LACK OF IT)

A photograph is a recording of light, and you'll quickly find that all light is not the same. Light can be bright and intense or it can appear soft and even. Color is transmitted through light, such as the reds and oranges of a sunset, or may disappear to black in the shadow of a tree. Light has an amazing variety of qualities to capture—here are three to look for out in the field.

Silhouetting

Silhouetting happens when your main light source is directly behind your subject matter. The background of your photo is exposed properly, while items closer to you turn dark from insufficient light.

A camera is not as capable as our eyes at seeing detail in both bright and dark areas at the same time. If you're shooting up at the bright sky without the flash on, your foreground subjects will go dark.

For this scene, a silhouette works beautifully.

Back Lighting

The light shining *through* a natural object is often more beautiful than the light shining directly on the subject.

The veins of the leaf and the petals of the flower become more striking when illuminated from behind.

Color Cast

At certain times of the day, light takes on different colors. The setting sun will give your subject a warm glow with yellow highlights and long shadows like the photo on the left. Photos taken in the shade of the bright morning sun will have a soft, even light with not much contrast, like the photo below.

When the sun is behind a cloud, it's a great time to take a portrait.

Looking into the sun often results in a spectacular burst of light and shadow. For another fun effect, hide the full blast of the sun behind a tree or mountain. Raise the exposure compensation ⊡ if the photo turns out too dark (pg. 13).

SHADOW PLAY

Shadows give objects shape and form. We sense the movement of time in the shadows, and rely on shadows to show us depth and distance. Let's face it, without shadows we'd be lost—and so would our photography.

IN THE FIELD

Time of Day

One way to make sure you get great shadows is to do your shooting late in the day or early in the morning. When the sun is at a low angle in the sky, it casts long shadows. The light is also more colorful when it travels through more of the atmosphere, bouncing off all those tiny dust particles.

IN THE FIELD

Shadoette

Combine a silhouette (pg. 44) with a shadow to create an interesting shadoette. (I just made a new word. Quick—somebody call Mr. Webster.)

How would this pumpkin look without a shadow? You guessed it...not so photo worthy.

Long shadows on the beach...that's what memories (and cheesy postcards) are made of.

TO FLASH OR NOT TO FLASH?

That's the question. Most of the time, your camera makes good decisions in automatic mode. However, certain lighting situations can be tricky for your camera. Here are three instances where manual adjustments to the flash can help your camera in times of distress.

IN THE FIELD

Light in the Shadows

Most people wouldn't think of using their flash in the middle of a sunny day. However, direct overhead light produces dark shadows and bright highlights. Using the flash in this situation helps to brighten the shadows and bring more evenness to the photo.

The shadows are too dark in the photo above. The flash helps brighten the dark shadow areas which results in a much better photo.

1 Switch to Automatic mode 📷. Open the camera's flash if necessary.

2 Use the viewscreen to make sure the Flash mode is set to normal. Push the flash button until this symbol appears .

3 Take the photo and preview ▶ your results.

Window Flash

When taking a photo indoors in front of a window, use flash to light your subjects. This will balance the light flooding in from the window.

Before turning on the flash, this innocent hug looked more like a scene from a horror movie.

Flash Power

If your flashed photo is too light or too dark, you might be able to adjust the flash power on your camera.

The normal flash setting was not powerful enough to reach through this stack of tires.

1 Access your camera's programmable features and look for a Flash setting.

2 Set the power to low or high, depending on your needs. The flash icon may show up with a plus or minus sign next to it after you do this ⚡.

3 Retake the photo and compare the results in Preview mode ▶.

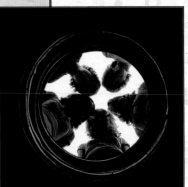

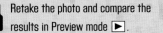

FLASHY EFFECTS

Flash photography with a small digital camera can result in an ugly photo. Dark backgrounds, weird shadows, and demon posessed people are just a handful of the problems you might encounter. That said, if you know what you're doing, the flash can make for surprisingly cool photos.

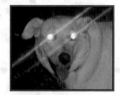

Flash will reveal that your pet is an alien with mutant powers!

IN THE FIELD

A Star is Born

Bright lights, big city...or small-town movie theater. Here's an example where the flash really shines. Take your camera with you to the local movie theater. On your way to get tickets, take a few flash photos in front of a lighted display using the steps below.

1 Switch the camera to Automatic mode and turn on the flash .

2 Position your subject 5 or 6 feet from the flashing movie poster.

3 Position yourself and the camera at least an arm's length from the subject.

4 Frame the shot so that the subject's face is framed by the flashing lights. Take the photo.

5 Preview ▶ the photo and make adjustments if necessary. The two most common problems are solved on the left.

Is the flash is too bright on the subject?
Take one step back and zoom in to get the same cropping. If that doesn't work, lower your flash power by one step (pg. 49).

Are the lights in the background too dim?
Move everyone closer to the display.

In the photo above, the auto-flash isn't powerful enough to light the background at this restaurant. Also notice that items in the foreground receive most of the light and cast annoying shadows (like the ketchup bottle).

Soft flash was used in the photo on the right to capture everything in the restaurant with an even light. The ketchup bottle shadow is still there, but not as noticeable.

Soft Flash

Some cameras come with a soft flash setting that will expose correctly for the background light, and then flash the foreground. This helps the light look more natural. The only hangup is that you might get camera shake (pg. 15). Hold your camera still and ask your subjects not to move.

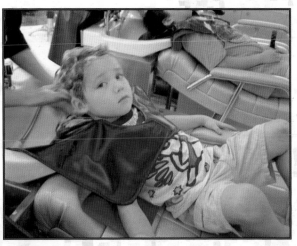

Soft flash was the perfect choice for this beauty parlor shot. Everything in the photo is evenly exposed. There are no hard shadows, so the natural mood of the setting isn't disturbed (only your little brother is).

CHAPTER 4
composition

...where you'll find
the secrets to taking
great photographs.

oto ▶
madness

COMPOSITION NUTRITION

Composition is a term used to describe how the parts of a photograph work together in forming the whole. Taking a good photo takes time, energy, and a bit of creativity. So how do you do it? Here are some tips to help you compose good photos.

IN THE FIELD

Don't Be Lazy

Work your way around a subject to see what's the best angle and framing. After you take the first photo, try to improve on it by moving to a different viewpoint. Keep moving around and changing your perspective until you've got the best shot possible. With a digital camera, you can take as many photographs as you need— simply delete the extras.

IN THE FIELD

Be Sensitive to Balance and Eye Movement

Our eyes like to see balance in the elements of a photograph. In terms of color, this photo has a good balance between light and dark color regions. Squint your eyes and the distinct regions will become more apparent. (To learn more about color in composition, check out Chapter 3.)

Our eyes also like to move around a photograph. The diagonal lines in this photo—formed by the edge of the umbrella, the shovel, and the shadow—move our eyes to different areas of interest. (To learn more about lines in composition, turn to page 60.)

How do the key elements of this photo relate to the grid lines?

Play by This Rule

The Rule of Thirds is a very useful rule of composition. It'll help you arrange elements inside the frame in a way that's pleasing to the eye. The Rule of Thirds works because our eyes naturally gravitate toward a two-thirds division of an object or space.

To practice this rule, imagine that lines divide the viewfinder into three horizontal and three vertical sections (like the white lines I've drawn on the photos here). Now arrange the elements of your photograph to correspond with the imaginary grid. You can place objects directly on the lines, or use objects to fill the imaginary boxes. For example:

Got a horizon? Place it on either of the horizontal grid lines.

See a building? Put its edge on a vertical line.

Taking a portrait? Put the eyes on a line.

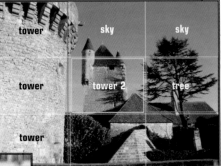

See how easy it is to play by the rules?* In fact, you may have already been following this rule—take a look at your photo collection. Are you a subconsious composition genius?

*Once you've figured out the Rule of Thirds, don't be afraid to break it. (This applies to all rules, especially the one about not eating ice cream for breakfast.)

SEEING IS BELIEVING

Our brains record the world much differently than a camera. We can be very selective about what we *choose* to see, focusing our attention on one object and ignoring everything else. A camera, however, cannot ignore what it "sees"—it'll record everything that's in the frame. That's why taking a *great* photo is so hard! *See* for yourself.

The skater above has to compete for your attention with the the fence and background. By pointing the camera in a different direction, the sunlit skater on the left pops out of the dark shady background (and almost out of his pants).

IN THE FIELD

Clean up the Clutter

■ What's included in the frame? Is your main subject dominant? Simplify your image before you take the picture.

■ Move yourself or your subject to a less distracting environment to get a cleaner background.

Skysolation

One way of simplifying a photo is to isolate the subject matter, and there's no better place than the big blue yonder. Looking up from below removes distracting elements from the background and increases the impact of your subject. Use skysolation to make your photographs larger than life.

Even in Black & White, skysolation gets the job done.

This lighthouse looks majestic in the airy blue sky. Notice how the repeating elements and diagonal lines move your eye up and down the photograph.

Unforeseen Images

Images are a form of communication, and you have to be extra careful to not accidentally communicate something absurd. For instance, did the photographer really mean to turn Dad into a reindeer?

Challenge your brain to do more with less.

JUST CROP IT

Unlike our own vision, the camera sees the world through a limited window. Deciding what goes in that window—and what gets left out—is a stimulating process for the brain. If your brain isn't delighted with what you see, creative cropping can help. Crop it **IN THE FIELD** or **IN THE LAB**.

IN THE FIELD

Force Fit

Sometimes you can't capture everything you want in one shot without turning the camera at an angle. It's quite alright—in fact, it might make your shot more interesting than a standard view.

Give the camera a twist. When your brain says, "Hey, that's cool," take the shot.

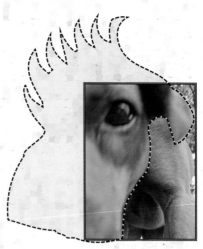

Making sense out of images is fun. Is this a brown wooly elephant or an out-of-focus cockatoo eating on some fried chicken? Mmmm...fried chicken.

IN THE LAB

Brain Teaser

Our brains like a good challenge. When something isn't immediately recognizable, it holds our attention. You may already have a photo that you can make more interesting by cropping or rotating it.

1 Open an image that doesn't tickle your fancy in its present state.

2 Crop and rotate your image so that it becomes more interesting to you. It may look best cropped to a bookmark shape (below) or rotated to an unnatural orientation (left).

Rotate

Crop

A beautiful desert landscape framed by two window openings.

THE FRAME GAME

Photographs can have more than one frame or bounding box. Anything that encloses a space is already a visual frame. And you can frame the frame! The more you look, the more you'll find that the world around you has all kinds of framing opportunities.

Frames don't always have to be square. This cement pipe makes an interesting frame. The abstract background adds a bit of intrigue.

Hocus Focus

When playing the frame game, where to focus becomes an issue. Focusing on a frame at a close distance to the camera (1 to 8 feet) will usually result in a blurry background. If you want everything to be in focus, move farther away from the frame and zoom in to crop.

You can have other items in the photo beside the frame, like this giant pot at the Forbidden City.

Straighten Up

After taking a shot with horizontal or vertical lines, you might find that some of the lines don't appear straight. Your basic software package probably has a tool to fix this problem.

Sharpness: 0
Straighten: -1.2

Some software places a grid over your image to help you get straightened out.

When your eyes move around this photo, the magnetic power of lines pull them back to the center. Even the spaces between the lines lead to the focal point.

LINE LANGUAGE

Lines are powerful design elements. They break up spaces, create shapes, and draw our eyes along their paths. Lines can communicate stability or imbalance, imply movement or stillness. You'll find there's no end to the creative potential of lines.

IN THE FIELD

Finding Lines

Look for lines whenever you're out shooting. Here are some ideas:

- Cities and buildings
- Streets and lane markings
- Natural objects, like trees
- The veins of a leaf
- Cracks in surfaces
- Ropes and cables
- Shadows and windows

IN THE FIELD

Help, the Sky is Falling!

Turn your camera at an angle and see what happens. Your picture will take on a whole new meaning. It might even turn a still scene into an action-packed moment. A horizon that's not horizontal adds wacky elements of instability and motion to your photo.

This parking garage looks more like an elevator shaft from this angle.

IN THE LAB

Leading Lines

See if you can trace your eye movement as you look at the photograph on the left. Do your eyes follow the lines? Which lines do your eyes gravitate toward the most? Do your eyes stop at any location along their path?

Pst! Here's a hint.
Now look at other photographs and observe how lines move your eye around the frame.

PANORAMIC PICTURES

Some situations are impossible to capture through the viewfinder—it's just not wide enough. By taking photos in sequence, you can extend your field of view and build a panoramic image.

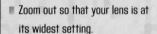

Capturing Images in Sequence

Check your camera for a panoramic setting. It can help you overlap sequential photos and stitch them together right on the camera.

No panoramic setting? No worries. You can stitch your photos in the lab. Use the tips on the right for capturing your images:

- Zoom out so that your lens is at its widest setting.

- Use the same exposure setting for each image in the sequence.

- Keep your horizon level (it's harder than you think). Use a tripod for serious landscape panoramas (pg. 15).

- Overlap your images 25 to 40 percent. Stitching software will do a better job with more overlap (40 percent or more).

- Take the sequence more than once, especially if there are people or moving objects in the photo.

Rotate your camera like this to overlap sections of your photo sequence.

If you don't have stitching software, print your images and assemble a panoramic collage like the one above.

IN THE LAB

Stitching Software

If you're lucky, your software has a panoramic stitching feature that you can use to compile multiple photos into one seamless image.

1 Open the panoramic feature of your software and choose the image files to be compiled.

2 Drag the images to the window in the correct order. Overlap the images and rotate them if necessary with the tools provided (**A**).

3 Click OK to build the panorama. Crop it to your liking (**B**).

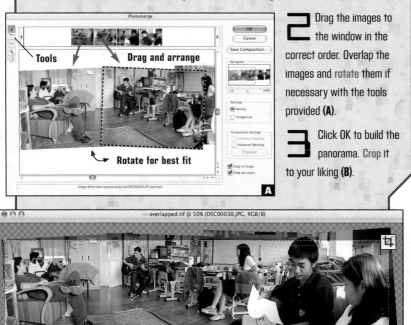

CHAPTER 5
macrotopia

...because there's a wild world of close-up photography to explore.

oto
madness

FLOWER POWER

The Macro icon is a flower for a good reason. Flowers are some of the coolest subjects to get close to. They come in an amazing variety of colors and shapes, and up close they look like tiny worlds of their own.

If I were an insect, this would be my favorite landing pad.

IN THE FIELD

Hocus Focus

You don't always have to focus on the item closest to the lens. Blurry objects in the foreground can create a sense of depth.

1 Set your camera to Macro mode ✿.

2 Go into your camera settings and switch the focus setting to center-weighted [○].

3 Point the center of the frame to the item you wish to focus on. Halfway depress the shutter button to focus (**A**), then shift the frame to your desired composition (**B**) and shoot!

Brightness:	
Contrast:	
Saturation:	
Temperature:	
Tint:	
Sharpness:	
Straighten:	
Exposure:	

IN THE LAB

Color Crazy

1 Open a colorful flower image for editing.

I adjusted the Temperature and Tint sliders to change the color of these flowers.

2 Play with the color settings until the flower takes on a new look (see above). Save the image with a new name.

3 Re-open the original image and repeat step 2 until you have four completely different photos.

The original image.

4 Import your new images to a word-processing or layout program, and arrange them in a grid. Then print all four as one photo.

Hue:	+96
Saturation:	+11
Lightness:	+3

The flowers to the left were made by shifting the color spectrum with the Hue slider.

TOO CLOSE FOR COMFORT

When the camera gets very close to a face, strange things start to happen: noses get bigger, necks and foreheads shrink, and every pore and hair stands up and says, "Hello!" This could get very dangerous with the wrong person in front of the camera.

Gabriella is hard to recognize at this distance— unless you know that she always wears two different colored contact lenses.

IN THE FIELD

Getting Close

To get as close to your subject as possible, set your lens to its widest setting (zoom out). This will allow more light into the lens and help to avoid camera shake (pg. 15).

1 Set your camera to Macro mode 🌷.

2 Make sure you have enough light on your subject. Change locations if you need better light.

3 Place the camera very close to your subject and lightly push the shutter button to pre-focus. Use viewscreen to see if your subject is in focus. If she's not, move yourself back a tiny bit and refocus.

4 Hold the camera as still as you can and take the photo. For tips on stabilizing the camera, see page 15.

I had to shine a reading lamp directly into Phoebe's face to take this shot without using the flash. Luckily, she didn't mind being in the spotlight.

IN THE LAB

Mad Scientist

Combine different sections of your close ups to create a new creature. Now that's a real catwoman. Meow.

A

B

1. Place the photos you wish to combine into a word-processing or layout program.

2. Use the **Crop** tool to remove a section of the first image (**A**).

3. Overlap your images, then use the **Resize Handle** to scale the facial features to match one another (**B**).

LOL—you know you want to!

Resize Handle

MINIATURE LANDSCAPES

For this activity, imagine that you're an ant or a small mouse.
What would the world look like? A rock might look like a
boulder and a patch of grass could become a dense forest.
Use your imagination and your camera to capture the beauty
of being small.

IN THE FIELD

Shrink Yourself

1 Walk around and think small. What
would be an awesome landscape to a
very small creature?

2 Frame different perspectives of the
scene using the viewscreen. Watch
out for anything that gives away the true size of the landscape.

3 Experiment with the focus. How does it change the scene when
the focus is closer or farther away? Have fun and take lots of
photos. There will be a few that stand out when you get back to the lab.

Is this a sandy
gully or a forboding
mountain range?
It depends on your
perspective.

Don't walk through this jungle without protective clothing. (I guess that's why bugs wear their skeletons on the outside.)

IN THE FIELD

Hocus Focus

In Macro mode 🌷, the depth of focus is very narrow. Notice how the stalks of these "trees" fall out of focus as they get close to the lens. Also, the house in the background is way out of focus.

"Help! My spaceship has crashed-landed on an alien planet!"

Am I in a cave? Are these two-ton boulders or skipping stones from a creek bed? Only the photographer knows.

BUGGIN' OUT

Insects and other creepy crawlies make excellent subjects for Macro mode photography—assuming you can get the shot before they fly or crawl away.

This caterpillar was moved from her original setting to this bright red leaf for visual impact. Luckily, she wasn't very slimy.

This handrail is more like a mountain to this katydid. Notice how the lines in the photograph help tell the story by guiding the eye up the "mountain."

IN THE FIELD

Bug Catcher

1 Set your camera to Macro mode 🌷 and set your focus setting to center-weighted (pg. 68).

2 Determine how close you can get to your subject without disturbing its comfort zone. Try zooming in and taking a few photos from a safe distance before getting closer.

3 Focus on the bug, then quickly adjust the framing and composition to your liking (see Chapter 4). Take the shot before the bug slimes you.

Crop to Get Closer

Crop your macro shots to make them more interesting. Just make sure you take the photo at the highest megapixel setting (pg. 16).

1 Open your image for editing.

2 Select an area to crop.

3 Push the crop button.

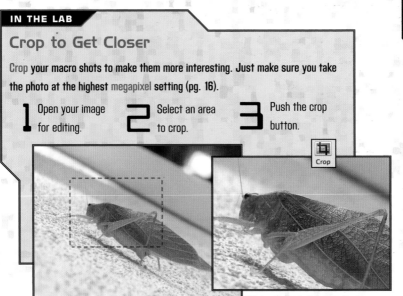

Crop

Now we're in his personal space.

Temperature Correction

In order to have enough light to record this shot, I had to shine a lamp on the Luna moth. However, the incandescent light cast a warm tone over my image. To correct the color back in the lab, I made a heavy adjustment to the Temperature slider toward the cool end. Then, to retain the nice brown fur colorings of the moth, I moved the Tint slider slightly toward magenta. Experiment with the temperature and tint of your pictures.

Temperature: ☀ ═◁▷═══════ ☀ −64.1

Tint: ◉ ═══◁▷══════ ◉ −13.6

DON'T FORGET THE DETAILS

When you're taking photos, don't get too caught up in the big picture and miss the details. Detail shots tell us stories that other photos can't. They get us close to texture, give us a sense of time and age, and give our imaginations a chance to extend outside the frame. Add detail shots to your image library and start telling the whole story.

IN THE FIELD

Finding Details

Look for details whenever you're out shooting. Here are some ideas:

- Textured walls
- Door knockers and windows
- People's hands
- Weathered objects
- Bark on trees
- Storefront signs
- Car grills

These door handles are very interesting. But so is the crackled paint, which you wouldn't be able to see at a distance.

IN THE LAB

Sharpen the Details

Use the Sharpness slider of your software to help sharpen the detail of your images. If you have advanced software, use Unsharp Mask to gain greater control. Don't go overboard though—too much sharpness looks unnatural.

| Sharpness: | | 54.4 |
| Straighten: | | 0 |

This beautiful detail of a lily pond uses the Rule of Thirds and leading lines (pgs. 55 and 61).

digital ph

superb subjects

...look here to find some great ideas for your next photo shoot.

oto madness

SELF PORTRAIT

Do you pretend to be window shopping, while you're really checking out your reflection? Admit it. You also like to look through friend's photo albums just to see pictures of yourself. We all do it—there's nothing better than a great photo of numero uno. So why not take your own? Here are a couple ideas.

Natural light is best for portraits—never flash. Take your shot beside a window for beautiful highlights and shadows.

IN THE FIELD

1 Switch your camera to Portrait mode 👤.

2 Get the camera out of your hands for formal-type shots. Holding the camera while shooting often results in awkward body positions. Use a tripod and the Timer Delay ⏱ (pg. 15).

3 Set the focal distance (pg. 13) or pre-focus on something the same distance as you will be to the camera.

4 Take the shot and check it for focus. Make adjustments if necessary.

Check your camera for built-in filter effects (pg. 83). Or wait untill you're in the lab to experiment (see below).

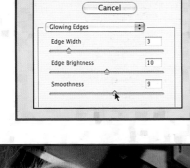

IN THE LAB

Deep Thoughts

Express more than the camera can record by adding special effects or filters to your image (pg. 106). If your software doesn't have filters, you may want to upgrade to one of the programs mentioned on page 21.

Glowing Edges (100%)

OK
Cancel

Glowing Edges

Edge Width	3
Edge Brightness	10
Smoothness	9

Filter   View   Window   Help

Artistic ►
Blur ►
Brush Strokes ►
Distort ►
Noise ►
Pixelate ►
Render ►
Sharpen ►
Sketch ►
Stylize ►   Diffuse...
Texture ►   Emboss...
Video ►   Extrude...
Other ►   Find Edges
                 Glowing Edges...
Digimarc ►   Solarize
                 Tiles...
                 Trace Contour...
                 Wind...

For a fabulous glamour shot, get your hair flying over an open vent.

This kitten wouldn't stay still for a photograph, so I turned on the flash and walked backwards with him while taking the photo.

CATS & DOGS

Here's your chance to experiment on someone who will love the extra attention—your pet! If you don't have one, find someone who does. Just make sure you've been properly introduced before sticking a camera in an animal's face.

Luke is happy to be in the woods, but he's not sure what to think about the camera.

IN THE FIELD

Eye Contact

Animal shots have a lot more impact when you're at their eye level. However, many dogs avoid eye contact, so if you want a shot of them looking at the camera, you have to be patient. Pre-focus and be ready for the exact moment to shoot.

This Boston Terrier was thirsty after his high-flying antics.

IN THE FIELD

Filter Modes

A lazy housecat makes for a great opportunity to experiment with camera settings.

1 To photograph using the available light, turn off the flash ⚡ (pg. 48).

2 Switch to Program mode and set the white balance to your light source (pg. 13).

Phoebe looks relaxed in Sepia.

The Posterize filter merges similar colors for an illustrated look.

3 If the viewscreen warns of possible camera shake, put the camera on the floor for stability (pg. 15).

4 Take the shot, and then preview it ▶. Check the focus and exposure.

5 If the image is too dark, adjust the exposure setting up a step or two (pg. 13).

6 Change the filter modes. Try Black & White, Sepia, Negative, and Posterize modes.

FABULOUS FIREWORKS

Fireworks are more fun to shoot than they are to watch. You need plenty of memory space, because catching a spectacular explosion takes a bit of trial and error—and there's no time to waste once they begin. Use the steps below and have a blast.

Including the crowd with the fireworks adds visual interest.

View the fireworks from a tall building and catch the city lights as well.

IN THE FIELD

Stop the Show

1 Set up your camera and tripod (pg. 15).

2 Switch your camera to Night mode 🌙 or Fireworks mode 🎆 if your camera has it.

3 Set your focal distance to infinity so that your auto-focus doesn't waste time trying to focus on the night sky. (Fireworks mode should handle this for you.)

4 Start taking photos of the fireworks. Save room on your memory card for the big finale—that's when you'll probably get your best shot.

FOCAL DISTANCE
Multi AF
Center AF
0.5 meters
1.0 meters
3.0 meters
7.0 meters
∞ Infinity ◁

If you don't have a tripod, rest your camera on the overpass rail to get this photo. I recommend wearing your camera strap.

IN THE FIELD

Fake Fireworks

If you can't wait for the fireworks, you can make your own using Night mode 🌙 creatively. Just find lights that are moving, such as car lights on a highway or night lights on a Ferris wheel (both pictured above). Even if you find an awesome set of colored lights that are stationery, you can swirl your camera around while taking the photo and create a dazzling display like the photo below.

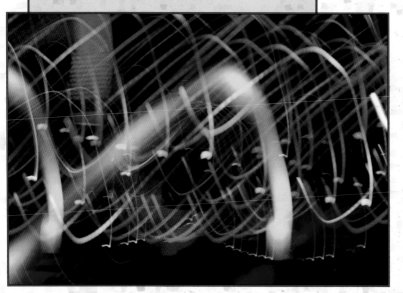

MUSEUM SHMUSEUM

Going to the museum doesn't have to be boring anymore—it can be a photographic opportunity. Many art museums will let you take photos inside as long as you follow their rules. Using your flash and carrying a tripod may be prohibited, so make sure you ask before doing either. Don't worry though, you can still walk away with some memorable photos.

You don't have to ask a statue's permission to take an absurd close-up.

IN THE FIELD

Art Thief

1 Turn off your flash 🚫. Not only does it damage the artwork—it can be annoying to other people.

2 Set your white balance setting to the correct light type for each situation you encounter (pg. 13).

3 Practice being your own tripod (pg. 15).

Glass Case

If you can see through glass, so can your camera. The trick is not seeing the reflection of you or the camera in the glass (pg. 99). The solution is to get as close to the glass as possible. You can even put your lens right on the glass. (Just cross your fingers that no alarms go off.)

Holding the camera lens against the glass also helps stabilize the camera and prevent camera shake (pg. 15).

When objects are at different depths from the camera, you can choose which one you want to have in focus (pg. 68).

Digital Haze

In low light situations, your camera may record an image that lacks in contrast and saturation. Don't dismay. You did a great job keeping the camera still and the image in focus. Your software can make up for the lack of light, and bring the WOW back to the artwork.

Use the Enhance feature of your software when an image looks drab.

Enhance

GOING FISHING

You don't need an underwater camera or an expensive trip to a tropical island—just take your digital camera to the aquarium. You're sure to find more than one fantastic photo opportunity. (And you can skip the gift shop, because when you get back to your photo lab, you can make your own cool stuff.)

The above photo was taken without a flash. It was enhanced with software in the lab (see the next page).

IN THE FIELD

Fish Flash

Don't let your camera take over and auto-flash the fish. You'll get a cooler shot if you turn off the flash ⚡ and put the lens right up to the glass.

Also, try experimenting with the white balance settings to achieve special effects (pg. 13).

Glass Cleaning

Thick glass, flourescent lighting, and water combine to make a very blue-green photo. Here's how to fix it.

1 Move the Temperature and Tint sliders toward warm colors and away from cool greens and blues (pg. 75).

Temperature: ☀ —————●——— ☀ 20.4
Tint: ◉ —●——————— ◉ -37.9

2 Next, adjust the contrast and the sharpness to your liking (pg. 77).

3 Save your spectacular image. If you want to use it to make awesome stuff, check out the idea below.

Make a Bookmark

1 Import your image to a word processing or layout program.

2 Crop the image to the shape of a bookmark. Then scale the bookmark to fit your favorite book (pg. 17).

3 Add a border if you like. Use a color from within the photo to accent the border.

Copy and paste as many bookmarks as you can onto the page before printing.

SUPERMAN CITYSCAPE

Build an awesome panoramic image of a skyline from inside a building. Your friends will swear you were flying.

IN THE FIELD

Observation Deck

1 When you're in a big city, take a trip to one of the tallest buildings and pay to visit the observation deck. Go in the morning or late afternoon to get the best light.

2 Find a spot where the glass window is in the shade and the glass is relatively clean.

3 Use a tripod or set your camera on a stable surface (pg. 15). Place your lens as close to the glass as possible. Tips for shooting through glass are on page 87.

4 Set your lens to its widest setting (zoom out). Change to Landscape mode 🔺.

5 Use the Timer Delay ⏱ and take shots in sequence (pg. 64).

You don't need to go to these extreme lengths to capture a cityscape.

IN THE LAB

Putting it Together

1 Open the panoramic stitching feature of your software (pg. 65).

2 Follow the instructions for loading your images, then arrange them in order in the window provided.

3 Experiment with the options. For this image, I chose Perspective mode with Cylindrical Mapping. Your software may have similar features.

4 Click OK to build your panorama. Then use the Crop tool 🔲 to remove any unwanted areas (pg. 65).

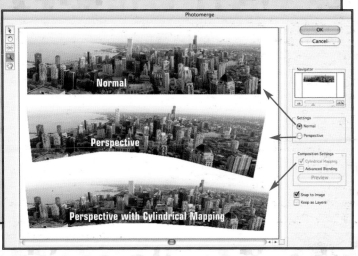

phunky fotos

...because there are so many fun pictures and crazy optical illusions out there.

oto ▶

madness

A small pond is a great place to catch a reflection that will turn the world upside down.

LIGHT BENDING

Reflections add a cool twist to a photograph. The subject matter is no longer just in front of the camera—it can be all around you. These photos give us a glimpse into the weirdness of reality, bending time and space. Here are a few ways to capture multiple realities.

Three unique worlds are captured in this photograph: light, shadow, and reflection.

IN THE FIELD

Finding Reflections

Look for these reflective surfaces:

- Car mirrors
- Lakes and ponds
- Aluminum foil
- Drinking glasses
- TV and computer screens
- Polished furniture
- Polished silverware
- Large glass windows

Combine reflection with night photography (pg. 28) to produce a dream-like effect. Can you get the same shot without seeing the camera in the frame?

IN THE FIELD

Hocus Focus

Focusing on reflective surfaces can be tricky. If your camera has a hard time focusing into a mirror, switch to Manual Focus. Experiment with the focal distance settings until you're satisfied with your shot (see the chart on page 84).

"So this is what I'd look like if I had a Siamese twin."

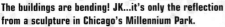

The buildings are bending! JK...it's only the reflection from a sculpture in Chicago's Millennium Park.

ARCHITECTURAL DETAILS

Seeing just one tiny part of a building can be just as interesting as seeing the whole thing. With the help of your zoom and some creative framing, you can produce an abstract masterpiece.

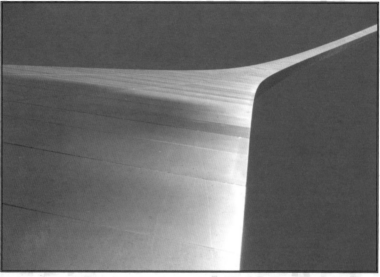

Is this a silver sidewalk in the sky or the Gateway Arch in St. Louis, Missouri?

Detail Shopping

1 Find a section of a building that intrigues you.

2 Set your camera to Landscape mode 🏔 and zoom in to the section of interest if you need to.

3 If your section has horizontal or vertical lines, make sure they are aligned with the frame.

4 Stabilize the camera (pg. 15), focus, and take the shot.

This Thai rooftop had many quirky horizontal lines. I did the best I could at making them straight with the frame, but some lines just aren't straight to begin with.

IN THE FIELD

The Melting Pot

Skyscrapers often have glassy exteriors that reflect other buildings. Catch them at daybreak or just before sundown for a spectacular melting effect. To learn more about reflections, see page 98.

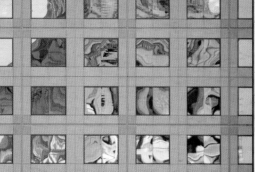

To get a straight shot like this, you must be at the same height as the center of the photo. The balcony of a building across the street would be a good choice.

"You're getting very sleepy...When I snap my fingers, you won't remember what this caption said."

This cute little girl is about to experience something frightening.

"Trust me... DON'T LOOK!"

MIRROR, MIRROR

Things can get pretty weird when mirrors aren't flat. Your arm might appear to have three elbows. Your legs might grow three times as long and look like toothpicks. And your face? Eww...a truck full of beauty supplies couldn't fix that. Look away! Look away!

You could become the newest member of the Fantastic Four.

"U... G... L... Y... I ain't got no alibi, I'm ugly. Absolutely ugly."

IN THE FIELD

Finding Weird Mirrors

Look for weird mirrors in these locations:

- Carnivals and fairs
- Children's museums
- Buses and trains
- Subways
- Funhouses
- Toy stores

The strongest gravity in the universe can be found near a Black Hole. These mirrors at the Chicago Planetarium gave us a glimpse at what we'd see entering a Black Hole. Somehow I don't think we'd be smiling.

IN THE FIELD

1 Find a mirror that has a curved surface or many dents.

2 Set your camera to Portrait mode 👤 and turn off the flash 🚫.

3 Switch to center-weighted focusing (pg. 68). Aim the focus at the object or person in the mirror and use the viewscreen to frame a funky photo.

4 Experiment with the position of the camera in relation to the mirror to get different effects. Refocus at each position before taking another shot.

5 After taking a few photos, take a close look at them in Preview mode ▶. Zoom in 🔍 and make sure your subject is in focus.

Let's go play some basketball.

Carmen's head grew three times its size thanks to this futuristic magnifying glass found at a Children's Museum.

HILARIOUS HAM

Why do so many of us go crazy in front of the camera? Maybe because we want the camera to record the side of us that's wild and fun to be around. Nobody wants to remember a sourpuss. Right? So let go—show your stuff. Trust me, these pictures will always make it into the photo album.

Here's a winning formula: upside-down glasses, colored braces, and a big open mouth.

IN THE FIELD

Soft Flash

When you're indoors, using the soft-flash setting will capture your subjects and record the background lighting. For more about flash photography, see pages 48 through 51.

Searching for intelligent life on the planet . . .

. . . .

. . . .

. . . .

Sorry, none found.

Coaching Kids

Sometimes it takes a bit of coaching to get your subjects to loosen up. You can turn it into a challenge—see who can make the funniest face. You could also offer a reward for the wackiest face. Usually a quarter or two will do.

These kids went from camera shy to all-out silly, with just a little coaching.

My breath must **REALLY** stink—even the dog is turning his nose!

COULD YOU REPEAT THAT?

Humans have used repeating patterns for ages as a way of unifying their designs. It works—just ask Mother Nature. You can create a sensational photo by capturing a pattern.

Patterns create a strong visual impact when they continue outside of the frame.

IN THE FIELD

Natural Inspiration

Nature is full of repeating elements, like the protective spikes on this cactus, or the scales of this snake. Use your zoom to get close to these patterns!

This cactus close up looks like a bird's-eye view of a miniature landscape (pg. 72).

These Chinese dragons don't have to be identical to create a pattern.

IN THE LAB

Pattern and Perspective

Repeating elements often form leading lines (pg. 62) that converge to the same point. Follow the lines (real or imaginary) to determine the point ● for each of the photographs here. There's only one correct point for each photo.

The light and shadows ● in this Black & White photo create a hypnotic pattern.

How did the architect know this building was going to look so cool at night? For ideas on taking night shots, see page 28.

IN THE LAB

Pattern Challenge

Here's a photo which has many repeating elements. There are also a number of unique elements that don't repeat. How many of each can you identify?

altered reality

...what can happen to your pictures with advanced editing software.

photo ▶

madness

FUN WITH FILTERS

Before the digital age, **filters** were placed in front of the camera lens to affect the lighting or change the color of a photo. Now computer filters can melt your mom's garden into a psychedelic lava lamp or shrinkwrap it in plastic. Just don't tell anyone how easy it is. They'll think you're an artistic genius.

Gaussian Blur

OK
Cancel
☑ Preview

− 17% +

Radius: 39.3 pixels

A

Hue: 0
Saturation: +82
Lightness: −9

B

IN THE LAB

Lava Lamping

1 Choose your favorite garden photo. If you don't have one, find a picture with lots of contrasting colors and shapes.

2 Open the Gaussian Blur filter (**A**). Blur your image so that all the detail becomes fuzzy.

3 Use the Hue/Saturation slider (**B**) to add saturation to the image until all the colors glow bright neon. Now, that would make a good desktop picture (**C**).

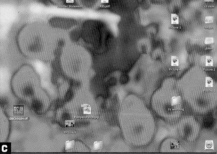

C

IN THE LAB

Same Photo, Different Filter

For the image on the right, I used the Stained Glass filter.

For the image below, I used the Plastic Wrap filter (**A**), then adjusted the Hue and Saturation sliders (**B**) to change the colors.

The Filter Gallery lets you choose between filters and preview their effects on your image.

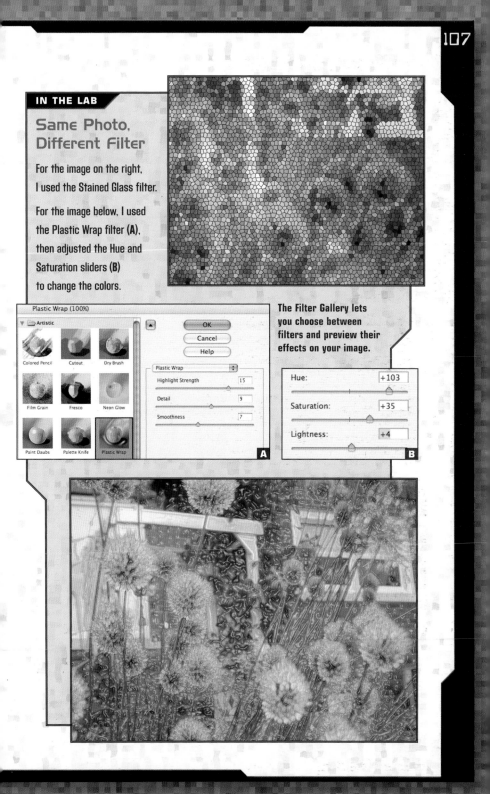

Plastic Wrap (100%)

▼ 🗀 Artistic

Colored Pencil Cutout Dry Brush

Film Grain Fresco Neon Glow

Paint Daubs Palette Knife Plastic Wrap

OK
Cancel
Help

Plastic Wrap

Highlight Strength   15
Detail   9
Smoothness   7

A

Hue: +103
Saturation: +35
Lightness: +4

B

KILLER KICKFLIP

This image was made by tweaking an architectural detail (pg. 96) and adding a silhouette (pg. 44).

IN THE LAB

Making the Background

1 Open an architectural detail shot that has many horizontal and vertical lines **(A)**.

2 Apply a filter to the image. I chose **Distort / Polar Coordinates (B and C)**.

Filter	View	Window	Help
Artistic	▶		
Blur	▶		
Brush Strokes	▶		
Distort	▶	Diffuse Glow...	
Noise	▶	Displace...	
Pixelate	▶	Glass...	
Render	▶	Ocean Ripple...	
Sharpen	▶	Pinch...	
Sketch	▶	Polar Coordinates...	
Stylize	▶	Ripple...	
Texture	▶	Shear...	
Video	▶	Spherize...	

B

Polar Coordinates

OK
Cancel

50%

◉ Rectangular to Polar
○ Polar to Rectangular

C

3 Next, adjust the hue and saturation of the image to your liking (pg. 39). Make it wild and crazy.

Adding the Silhouette

4 Open the silhouette and use the Magic Wand tool ✎ to select a dark area. Hold the Shift key and click on any other dark areas to add them to the selection (**D**).

5 Use the Move tool ⊹ to drag the selection to your other image. Alternatively, **Edit / Copy** the selection, then **Edit / Paste** it onto the other image. Either way, it should create Layer 1 above the colorful background.

6 Next, scale Layer 1 to a size that works well with the composition, using **Edit / Free Transform** or **Edit / Transform / Scale**. Hold the Shift key while you resize the layer to keep the proportions unchanged. Double-click on the image to set the transformation.

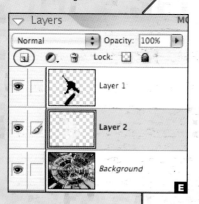

7 To add a glowing effect to the silhouette, select the background layer and click the new layer button on the layer window (**E**). Now choose a Paintbrush ✎ with a soft edge (**F**) and paint around the edges of your silhouette with a light color. Lower the opacity of Layer 2 to help blend it with the background.

Here's another image created from the same two photos. Didn't I tell you the possibilities are endless?

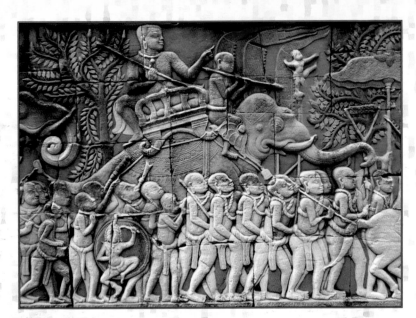

WHAT A RELIEF!

Many museums have ancient relief work from past civilizations. These stone monuments were often covered with dazzling color, but most of them have lost their decoration over time. Recreate the past and bring these ancient artifacts back to life.

IN THE FIELD

Shoot It

1 Go to an art museum (pg. 86). Look for a wall carving that tells a story.

2 Set your camera to capture the highest resolution possible (pg. 16).

3 Art museums may have a **NO FLASH POLICY**, so turn off your flash .

4 Look at the viewscreen and focus on the relief. If the image looks too dark, adjust the exposure ⊞ higher (pg. 13). If your image looks discolored from the lighting, adjust your white balance settings (pg. 13).

5 Stabilize your camera (pg. 15) and take the shot.

If you don't have photo software that allows you to paint over photographs, you can always do it the old-fashioned way by using tinting markers that are made for photographs.

IN THE LAB

Color It

1 Open the image with your image editing software.

2 If your image was shot in color, change the color to Black & White **(A)**. See page 41 for instructions.

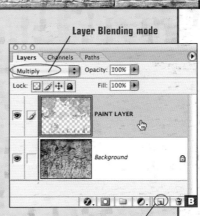

Layer Blending mode

3 Make a new layer above the main background to apply the paint. That way if you make a mistake, you can erase it without erasing the carving. Click on the New Layer button on the layer window **(B)**. Name the new layer "PAINT LAYER."

4 Change the Layer Blending mode of the PAINT LAYER to Multiply. This allows the highlight and shadow areas of the carving to show through the paint layer.

New Layer button

5 Select the Paintbrush tool and choose a brush size and a color from the brush menu. Paint areas of the relief different colors **(C)**.

6 If you make a mistake, switch to the Eraser tool and erase your mishap. Switch back to the Paintbrush tool to continue painting.

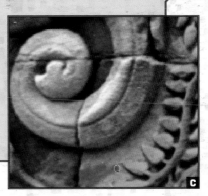

HELLO KITTY!

Remember the absurd close ups from page 70? Now combine the facial features into a truly magical creation.

Mastering the Lasso

Use Lasso tools to select an area for editing, copying, or moving. Three types of Lasso tools have been developed for different situations.

For freely tracing around an area, use the regular Lasso. Hold down the mouse button until you have fully enclosed what you want.

Use the Polygonal Lasso to select items with straight edges. Click to begin and click for each change in direction.

For items that have good contrast, use the Magnetic Lasso. It "sticks" to the edge of your object. Begin by clicking, and then let the computer find the edge as you move around the object. I love this tool.

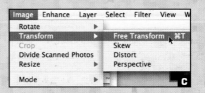

feathered edge

Pieces and Parts

1 Open both images with your advanced image editing software (pg. 20).

2 Click on the human image. Choose the Lasso tool and set the edge to feather 20 pixels. This will create a soft edge around the selection and help blend the two photos.

3 Trace around an eye **(A)**, then use the Move tool to drag the selection to the cat image. This will create a new layer.

4 Click on your new layer. Scale it to the correct size **(B)** with **Image / Transform / Free Transform (C)**. Rotate the feature if necessary. Double-click to set the transformation.

5 Repeat steps 2 through 4 with the other eye and the mouth. Try not to spit on the computer while laughing out loud.

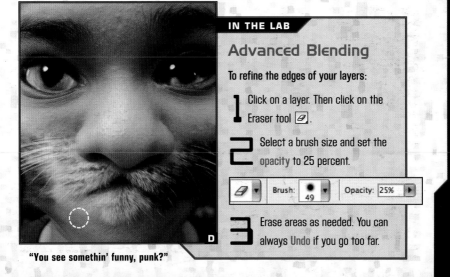

Advanced Blending

To refine the edges of your layers:

1 Click on a layer. Then click on the Eraser tool.

2 Select a brush size and set the opacity to 25 percent.

3 Erase areas as needed. You can always Undo if you go too far.

"You see somethin' funny, punk?"

GOOD OL' FASHIONED FACE LIFT

You can skip the photo shoot on page 42—just paste your face on an old photo to see what you'll look like as an old coot. Oh look, it's Skeeter and Granny Smith.

Funky Faces

1 Shoot funky face portraits of your friends. See page 94 for inspiration.

2 Find an old-timey portrait and take a photo of the photo with your camera. Lay it on a flat surface and use natural lighting.

A

Face Grab

This project begins with the same skills as the project on page 112. Select a face (**A**), move it to the old photo. Then scale it to the right size.

To get the faces the same color as the old Sepia, use the **Hue/Saturation** slider with the colorize box checked (**B**).

If the faces look too smooth on a grainy photo, use the Add Noise filter (**C**).

Finally, use the Eraser tool 🖉 to refine the edges of your new face (pg. 113).

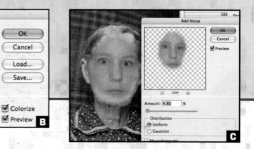

B

C

Use your face-snatching skills to swap heads. Then secretly pin the photo to a bulletin-board at your school for some good laughs.

HUMAN SPECIMEN

Ever wonder what happens to people after they're abducted by aliens? They go to the galactic zoo! This particular experiment observes the psychological effects on teenagers deprived of TV and the Internet. I think the blonde's already losing her cool.

IN THE FIELD

Gathering the Pieces

This experiment required three photos. For the background, I used a photo taken through glass at an aquarium (pg. 88). The next two photos were staged. For photo **A**, I had the subjects stand on a grassy hill and pose in different positions, like they were exploring their environment. For photo **B**, I had the subject stand behind a large piece of glass and act like she desperately wanted to get out.

IN THE LAB

Putting it Together

1 To remove the figures from the grassy backgroud, use the Magnetic Lasso tool to trace around them **(C)**. When you get to a corner spot, click the mouse button to set the point, then continue tracing. Finish the selection by clicking on the starting point.

2 If you need to add or subtract from the selection, change to the regular Lasso tool. Hold the Shift key while tracing to add to your selection. The Option or Alt key subtracts from your selection. To master the lasso, see page 112.

3 Once you have a figure selected, copy it using **Edit / Copy**. Then click on the aquarium image and chose **Edit / Paste**. This will make a new layer on top of the background **(D)**.

4 Repeat steps 2 through 4 for the other human specimens. Then use **Image / Transform / Free Transform** to scale each of the layers and place them in their spot. Double-click to set the transformation.

IN THE LAB

Advanced Blending

5 To complete the illusion, use the Burn tool to create shadows on the background layer and on the figures **(F and G)**. The Burn tool works like a paint-brush, but instead of painting a new color over the image, it darkens or burns the existing colors. You can specify whether it burns highlight, midtone, or shadow information. In this case, burning the midtones got the job done.

REFLECTING POOL POSTCARD

Create a cool reflection of a skyline and add jazzy text effects
to make a slick-looking postcard. Print the results on photographic
card stock and you're in business.
Now all you need is a stamp.

IN THE LAB

False Reflections

1 Select the area that you want to
reflect **(A)**. Copy and Paste it to a
new layer.

2 Click on Layer 1 and choose **Image / Rotate /
Flip Vertical** from the top menu **(B)**.

3 Double-click the Background layer to unlock it,
otherwise you won't be able to move it. Rename
it Layer 0 and click OK. Then use the Move tool 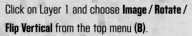 to
arrange the layers so they look like a reflection.

4 Click on Layer 1. Double-click on the Wave filter from the Styles and Effects window, or choose **Filters / Distort / Wave** from the file menu **(C)**. Fine tune the effect in the pop-up window so that your reflecting layer looks like waves on water.

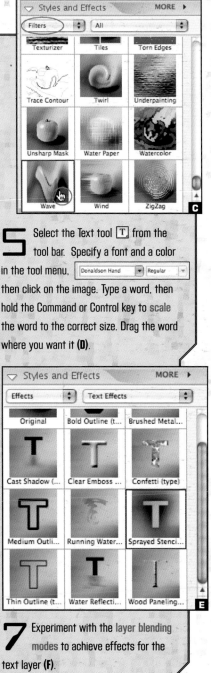

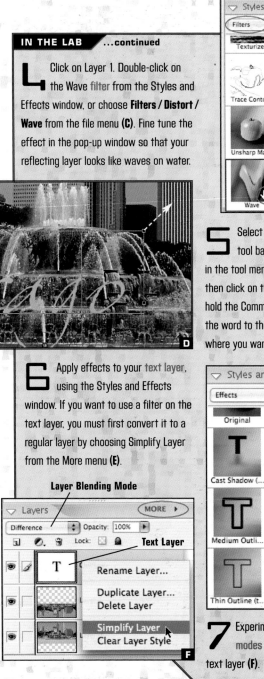

5 Select the Text tool [T] from the tool bar. Specify a font and a color in the tool menu, Donaldson Hand | Regular then click on the image. Type a word, then hold the Command or Control key to scale the word to the correct size. Drag the word where you want it **(D)**.

6 Apply effects to your text layer, using the Styles and Effects window. If you want to use a filter on the text layer, you must first convert it to a regular layer by choosing Simplify Layer from the More menu **(E)**.

Layer Blending Mode

Text Layer

Rename Layer...
Duplicate Layer...
Delete Layer
Simplify Layer
Clear Layer Style

7 Experiment with the layer blending modes to achieve effects for the text layer **(F)**.

GALACTIC WORMHOLE

Not all deep holes in the ground lead to China. Some transport you to other parts of the galaxy. Go ahead, jump right in...if you dare.

Gathering the Pieces

This experiment requires two cool photos. One is a photo taken through a tunnel, and the other is a night shot that has many points of light. The night shot was easy with Night mode 🌙 (pg. 28). For the tunnel, we went to a playground and peered through a stack of tires. It took some experimenting with the flash and the camera position to finally get the shot (pg. 49).

IN THE LAB

Creating the Wormhole

1 Use **Filters / Blur / Radial Blur** on the photo of the city lights **(A)**. The blur method I used was Zoom, but you can also Spin around the centerpoint. Specify the centerpoint of the effect by clicking inside the Blur Center Window. Click OK.

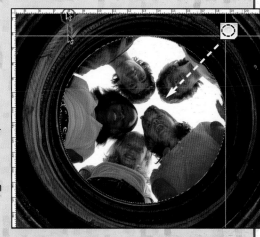

2 Use the Move tool to drag the tire photo over the city photo. Scale the layer if needed with **Image / Transform / Free Transform** (pg. 113).

3 Turn on your Rulers with **View / Rulers**. Drag a horizontal and vertical guideline from the ruler to the edge of the circle **(B)**.

4 Select the Elliptical Marquee tool. Set the edge to feather 20 to 30 pixels Feather: 20 px. Drag a selection from the intersection of the horizontal and vertical guidelines **(B)**.

5 **Edit / Copy** and **Edit / Paste** the selection. It should appear as Layer 2.

6 Select Layer 1 and change the Layer Blending mode to **Screen**. This will allow the lights from the Background to show through the dark areas of the layer **(C)**.

7 For the final touches, click on each layer and make adjustments to the color (see Chapter 3). Also experiment with the opacity of the layers.

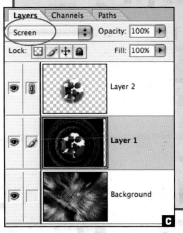

WILDER THAN WILD ANIMAL

Try your hand at making an animal extra distinctive. You can make decisions that nature would never make—like making this zebra look like a fruit rollup. I don't think he would last two seconds in the wild, but he'd look great in a zoo!

How wild can you make your animal?

IN THE FIELD

1 Choose an animal to photograph that has contrasting colors. If you're photographing a wild animal, please use all necessary caution.

2 Photograph the animal from several different angles. Try to simplify the background of your shots so that the animal really stands out (pg. 56).

3 If the background light is making your animal into a silhouette (pg. 44), you need to turn on the flash. However, this may scare your animal and disrupt your photoshoot.

IN THE LAB

1 Select the animal by tracing around it with a Lasso tool 🔍 (pg. 112). Copy and paste the selection and it will appear on a new layer. Name this layer ANIMAL LAYER by clicking on the layer title. (Later, when we apply a filter to the background it won't affect our animal because it's now a seperate layer.)

2 Add a new layer above the ANIMAL LAYER by clicking the New Layer button. Name it COLOR LAYER. Change the Layer Blending mode of this layer to Multiply. This will allow the natural shading of the animal to show through the COLOR LAYER.

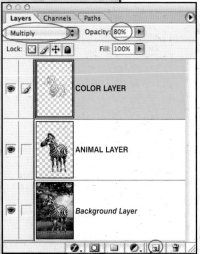

3 Click on the COLOR LAYER. Choose a small Paintbrush [Brush:] and a color from the tool pallete. Paint over the bright areas of the animal—in this case, the zebra's white stripes—with different colors. To make your paint job look more natural, lower the opacity of the COLOR LAYER.

New Layer button

4 Next, let's give the background some pizzaz by applying a filter. Select the Background Layer and choose a cool filter—I used the Radial Blur filter in spin mode (pg. 121).

Blank puzzle sheets are now made for desktop printers. Print your wild animal on a puzzle and give it to your friends.

Personally, I don't think you could top the work of my hairdresser— she's fabulous.

Megapixel Math

Use this chart to figure out how many pixels your camera records, and how big a print you can make at a GOOD QUALITY setting (pg. 17).

Camera	Digital Size (width x height = total pixels)			200dpi Print
0.3 megapixel	640 x 480	=	307,200	2 x 3 inches
1 megapixel	1152 x 864	=	995,328	6 x 4 inches
2 megapixel	1600 x 1200	=	1,920,000	8 x 6 inches
3 megapixel	2048 x 1536	=	3,145,728	10 x 7 inches
4 megapixel	2272 x 1704	=	3,871,488	11 x 8.5 inches
5 megapixels	2592 x 1944	=	5,038,848	13 x 10 inches
6 megapixels	2816 x 2120	=	5,969,920	14 x 10.5 inches

Acknowledgments

A big thanks to the Kids' Department at Lark Books for giving me this opportunity. My editor and good friend Rain Newcomb has been inspiring, patient, flexible, and fun. Thanks for the desk space.

I would like to thank the group of kids who modeled for this book and who put up with stupid requests I had of them. Special thanks to Anna and Sierra who contributed photographs to this book from their own photo collections. Their photos appear on pages 19, 43, 50, 81, 83, 85, 88, 89, 94, 95, and 114.

Some of the photos in this book were purchased for use from iStockPhoto.com. Kudos to all the great photographers who made it in the book. You made my job easier.

Also, I'd like to give a shout-out to all the ICS-Bangkok kids around the world, especially to those who found their way into my photo collection. We miss you all.

Glossary

Aperture. The opening in the lens that lets light into the camera.

Automatic color enhancement. An option on most software that improves the colors in a photo with a single click.

Available light. Light that is present without the use of a flash.

Camera shake. When the camera moves during a long exposure, resulting in a blurred image.

Center-weighted focusing. The camera focuses on whatever is in the center of the viewscreen.

Colorize. To shift all the color tones in a photograph toward one specific hue.

Color saturation. The intensity of a color.

Contrast. The degree of difference between tones of light and dark in a photograph.

Composition. How the elements of a photograph work together.

Crop. To cut away the edges of a photo.

Depth. The sense of distance between objects.

Depth of field. The region of a scene from foreground to background that appears in focus. A greater depth of field is achieved with a smaller lens opening. A shallow depth of field is achieved with a large opening.

Depth of focus. See Depth of field.

DPI. Dots per inch, the measurement that describes resolution.

Exposure. The amount of light a camera needs to record an image. An underexposed picture is too dark and an overexposed picture is too light.

Exposure compensation. A setting on the camera that will change how much light the camera lets in. Raise the adjustment to brighten a photo. Lower it to darken a photo.

Film. Something a digital camera will never need.

Film-speed equivalent. A number that indicates how fast the camera will record images. Use lower numbers for bright daylight and flash photos. Use higher numbers for low-light situations and action photos.

Filter. A setting either on the camera or in editing software that applies a cool effect to a photo.

Flash. A brief burst of light provided by the camera to properly expose a photo.

Focal distance. The distance from the camera to the subject of focus.

Focus. To adjust the camera so that the subject looks sharp and clear.

Frame. Anything that encloses or creates a boundary for an image.

Grayscale. A range of gray shades from white to black.

Horizon. The line where the sky and land (or water) appear to meet.

Hue. A word used to describe a specific color.

Image-editing software. Computer programs that alter digital photos.

Lasso. A tool that selects a certain part of an image for editing.

Layer. A feature of advanced photo software that overlaps photographs or pieces of photographs. Each layer can be manipulated independently from the other layers.

Layer blending mode. A menu on the layer window that specifies how a layer interacts with the layers beneath it.

Long exposure. When the camera takes more time to record an image.

Low light. When there is very little available light.

Manual focus mode. A setting that allows you to specify the focal distance.

Mega-pixel. A million pixels (roughly).

Pixel. The smallest building block of a digital image.

Pre-focus. Applying the auto-focus by pressing the shutter button halfway down. If you continue to hold the button down, you can reposition the subject of focus in the frame.

Portrait. A picture of a person.

Resize handles. In software, the points that appear around an image while scaling. Click and drag them to change the size of a photo. Hold the Shift key to retain the same proportions.

Resolution. The number of pixels per inch of photograph.

Rotate. To spin an image clockwise or counterclockwise around a center point.

Rule of Thirds. A rule of composition that lines up the subject matter on a grid.

Saturation. The intensity of a color.

Scale. To change the physical size of an image or layer.

Select. To single out one part of an image for editing or copying.

72 dpi. The ideal resolution for displaying images on a computer monitor.

Sharpen. To increase the difference between tones of light and dark in a photograph.

Silhouette. The dark shape and outline of an object that appears when the object is in front of a bright background.

Soft flash setting. A setting that exposes for the available light before flashing the foreground.

Temperature. The degree to which a photo appears cool (blue) or warm (red).

Tint. A shade or variety of color, on a scale from light to dark.

Tripod. A three-legged stand for supporting a camera.

Type layer. In advanced software, a layer of editable text.

- -

Undo. The best command ever. It restores the photograph to whatever it looked like immediately before the last thing you did to it.

Unsharp mask. An advanced sharpening filter that gives you greater control than a Sharpen slider.

- -

White balance. An adjustment for different lighting situations that may cast unwanted color on your image.

Metric Conversions

Inches	Centimeters
1 inch	2.5 cm
1.5 inch	3.8 cm
2 inches	5 cm
2.5 inches	6.4 cm
3 inches	7.6 cm
3.5 inches	8.9 cm
4 inches	10.2 cm
4.5 inches	11.4 cm
5 inches	12.7 cm
5.5 inches	14 cm
6 inches	15.2 cm
6.5 inches	16.5 cm
7 inches	17.8 cm
7.5 inches	19 cm
8 inches	20.3 cm
8.5 inches	21.6 cm
9 inches	22.9 cm
9.5 inches	24.1 cm
10 inches	25.4 cm
10.5 inches	26.7 cm
11 inches	27.9 cm
11.5 inches	29.2 cm
12 inches	30.5 cm
12.5 inches	31.8 cm
13 inches	33 cm
13.5 inches	34.3 cm
14 inches	35.6 cm

To convert feet to centimeters, multiply by 30.

Index